MISSEL THRUSH

Turdus viscivorus

KNOWN as the "Storm Cock" fr_____ flight. Called Missel Thrush (Mistle_____ _____sed liking for this berry, but doubt exist_____ _____ay to January this bird is to be seen on sea-clif__ _____, in woods, over open cultivated fields, or in hedge___ _____ng on worms, snails, grubs and berries. A restless, wander___ ___rd.

Mating and nesting may begin as early as January. A nesting site is sought in a wood, a row of trees along a hedge, or in a garden or orchard. Although the nest may be built close to a house, the bird is always wild and shy and is rarely seen except as he flies over the garden uttering his unmistakable note, or as he sits on the topmost branch of some tall tree and sings his love-song to his mate below. The song is wild, consisting of a somewhat incoherent medley of notes. The nest is placed on a horizontal branch of a tree some ten or twelve feet from the ground and often at some distance from the trunk. Very seldom is any other position chosen. The structure is fairly conspicuous: it has a foundation of mud and twigs, and is lined with grass and hay. Towards the end of February the hen may be incubating four to six eggs of a bluish colour with large reddish spots and blotches fairly evenly distributed over their surface.

The upper parts of the bird, in both sexes, is a uniform ash-brown; under parts buffish white, thickly spotted with dark brown. The young have the upper parts spotted with buff, and the spots below are smaller. Length 11 in.; wing 6 in.

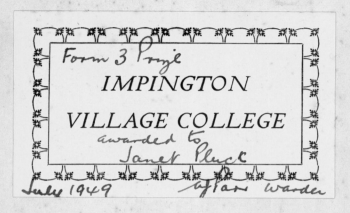

Form 3 Proje

IMPINGTON

VILLAGE COLLEGE

awarded to

Janet Pluck

July 1949   [signature] Warden

A POCKET-BOOK
OF
BRITISH BIRDS

Edited by

CHARLES A. HALL, F.R.M.S.

WITH 63 FULL-PAGE PLATES IN COLOUR
FROM BONHOTE'S "BIRDS OF BRITAIN"

A. & C. BLACK, LTD.
4, 5 & 6 SOHO SQUARE, LONDON, W.1

MADE IN GREAT BRITAIN

Text and colour plates printed by R. & R. CLARK, LTD., *Edinburgh*

Published Spring 1936

Reprinted 1939, 1942, 1944, 1948

PREFACE

FOR many years there has been a steady demand for Bonhote's *Birds of Britain*, which has been reprinted several times, but the recent increase of interest in Nature has caused a demand from field naturalists, ramblers, hikers, motorists, etc., for volumes which are readily carried in the pocket or knapsack. This book is a response to this demand. The Publishers have selected sixty-three of the plates from the larger volume by which sixty-eight species of birds are illustrated.

The plates are accurate in line and colour, and the notes which accompany them are, in the main, condensations from Bonhote's text, with some emendations and slight additions. The illustrations alone should enable the reader to identify the species seen in the field, but he will find the notes more than valuable, as they call attention to the salient features of the birds described and to points which might be overlooked in glancing at the plates. In addition, some observations are made in each instance on the haunt of the species, its habits, food, nest and eggs.

CONTENTS

Contents—*Continued*

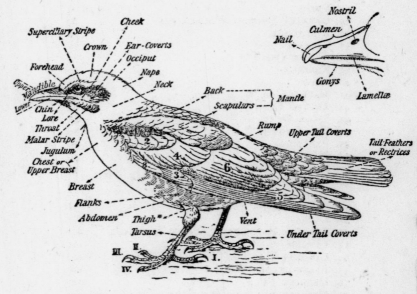

DIAGRAM SHOWING THE TOPOGRAPHY OF A BIRD.

WING. {
1. Lesser Coverts.
2. Median   „
3. Primary   „ } Greater or Major
4. Secondary „ }   Coverts.
5. Primaries } Quills, Remiges, or
6. Secondaries }   Flight feathers.
7. Bastard-Primary.
8.   „   Wing.
}

LEG. {
Tarsus.
Ist or hind toe.
IInd or inner toe.
IIIrd or middle toe.
IVth or outer toe.
}

* This joint is the heel proper, but is commonly called the thigh.

A POCKET-BOOK OF BRITISH BIRDS

SONG THRUSH

Turdus musicus (Linnæus)

ALSO known as the Mavis, or Throstle. This melodious British resident haunts any sort of cultivated country: broad fields, scanty hedgerows, the carefully cultivated garden of the wealthy, or the dusty plot of the town-dweller. Its food consists chiefly of insects, though worms are eaten freely and snails are a welcome delicacy. The bird may be seen hopping down the garden path with peculiar sidelong leaps, now and then varied by two or three quick short steps as he carries a snail to a smooth stone on which it is beaten till the shell is smashed: this accomplished, the snail is swallowed with a quick gulp.

By the end of March, even earlier, the nest may be found in the fork of some tree or bush, or on the beam of some outhouse—perhaps in the middle of a hedgerow, or occasionally on the ground. It is composed of rough grass and bents, and lined with mud pressed round and smoothed to form a fairly deep cup. The five eggs are a beautiful pale blue, with a few small black or purplish-mauve spots towards the larger end, these markings being in some cases entirely lacking. Incubation is carried on by the hen alone, but both birds take part in feeding the young.

The general colour of the bird above, including mantle and wings, is olive-brown, some of the major and median coverts having buffish tips. Breast yellowish, spotted with triangular olive-brown spots, the flanks uniformly olive, chin and throat white, margined with a row of dark streaks. Belly white. Bill brown. Legs pale flesh. Length 9·0 in.; wing 4·6 in. Young birds are spotted on the upper parts.

3

SONG THRUSH (*Turdus musicus*)

Adult (left and centre) FIELDFARE (*Turdus pilaris*) Young (right)

4

FIELDFARE

Turdus pilaris (Linnæus)

THIS bird may be confused with the Missel Thrush, but its grey
rump in contrast with its dark wings and tail is a conspicuous
feature, and it is smaller. It is a northern species which breeds
throughout Scandinavia, Russia and Siberia, as far east as the
Lena. In winter he migrates southward. In England his "chack,
chack" is heard towards the end of October, his numbers being
augmented as northerly blasts drive his kind farther and farther
south. While with us, he attaches himself to wandering flocks of
Missel Thrushes and Redwings. Thus he wanders the whole winter
through, feeding chiefly on the hips and haws in the hedges, and
probably also on worms and grubs, for he may frequently be met
with in ploughed fields.

Sexes alike in plumage, but the female is rather paler. The adult
male in winter has the head and neck slate grey, the feathers of
the crown having dark centres which are hardly noticeable at this
season; mantle and scapulars deep rufous brown; wing coverts
less rufous and showing traces of paler tips. Rump grey; quills and
tail dark brown. Fore-neck pale yellow, streaked with dark brown
on the sides; chest rufous streaked with brown; flank feathers dark
brown with broad white margins concealing the darker colour.
Lower breast and chest white. Legs and feet dark brown. Total
length 10 in.; wing 5·5 in.

This species is generally distributed throughout the British
Isles from October to May. Its winter migrations extend throughout the whole of Southern Europe and Asia Minor, including both
sides of the Mediterranean basin.

BLACKBIRD

Turdus merula (Linnæus)

ALSO called Black Thrush and Merle. Partially migrant. We see this bird mingling with Song Thrushes on the lawn. Towards the end of February his clear flute-like notes will be heard from the shrubbery or hedgerow—a song more mellow in tone but shorter and more monotonous than that of the Song Thrush. The food consists of worms, snails, slugs, spiders, insects and their grubs. In winter various berries are eaten.

The nest is built low down in some bush or hedgerow, on the ground in a bank, in a furze bush or on a heath, and is formed entirely of grass and bents, with a little mud for the foundation, but well lined with finer bents. The eggs, four to six in number, have a pale-blue colour, thickly mottled with reddish markings, sometimes uniformly distributed over their surface, at others confined to broader blotches forming a ring round the larger end, or, in some cases, the markings may be entirely absent. The young are fed almost entirely on earthworms, though insects are eaten.

In September and October large numbers leave our shores: many, however, remain, spending the winter in thick hedgerows, shrubberies and woods, or anywhere there is a bush high enough to give shelter. The Blackbirds found migrating along our shores are either surplus population driven farther afield by competition or wanderers from the colder north of Europe.

The male is a uniform deep glossy black, with bright orange bill. Young males in their first winter have a black bill. The female is of a uniform dull sooty brown above; chin greyish, with dark brown streaks. Chest reddish-brown, each feather with a darker tip, giving a mottled effect. The young generally resemble the female, but the feathers of head and back have light shafts.

Adult male (centre)   BLACKBIRD (*Turdus merula*)   Adult female (right)   Young (left)

8

Male (right)   STONECHAT (*Pratincola rubicola*)   Female (left)

STONECHAT

Pratincola rubicola (Linnæus)

BRITISH resident. This bird may be seen, summer or winter, on any rough common where furze or tangles of bramble form almost the only cover. When approached, he will rise and settle on the topmost spray of some furze bush, or possibly on the tall stem of grass or thistle. Jerking his tail with a quivering movement, or uttering his little call of "Tick, tick," he will move ahead with dipping flight to some other point of vantage as you approach, and display as he does so the white on his tail and wings. His food consists chiefly of insects and larvae. He mates and nests early in April: the nest, loosely built of grass and moss and lined with hair, is well concealed, being placed near the ground in the centre of a clump of furze or bramble. The five or six eggs are pale blue, speckled with rusty brown at the larger end. The male does not sit, but is always to be seen in the vicinity of the nest, continually bringing tit-bits to his mate. Both parents tend the young with great care, and after they have left the nest the family may often be found wandering about together, the male on the approach of danger sitting on the topmost spray of some bush while his family remain concealed under cover.

The plumage of the young is brown. The full-grown female resembles the male, except that the colouring is less brilliant, and the white markings are not so conspicuous. In the male, the head, throat and back are black; a patch on either side of the neck is white; tail and wings dark brown with a bold white patch on the wing coverts; breast and under parts bright rufous, lighter on the abdomen. The female has the upper parts striped with brown and the throat spotted with black. Length 5 in.; wing 2·55 in.

ROBIN
Erithacus rubecula (Linnæus)

BRITISH resident, common throughout the country. Of all our British birds, none perhaps has gained so complete a hold upon our imagination as the Robin, or Redbreast. He appeals deeply to our sympathy. He is a welcome guest in every home in the kingdom, and acknowledges the compliment by trusting us as few birds do. Perhaps it is in winter we know him best; however cold and stormy the weather, he always seems happy, cheerful and sprightly as he hops along the garden path or seeks his breakfast at the dining-room window. He is pugnacious, and other birds live in awe of him. He feeds on small worms, spiders, insects, grubs, soft fruits, berries and seeds, and household scraps in winter.

The nest is generally made in some hole in a bank or wall, at no great height from the ground, and concealed with considerable care. It is chiefly composed of moss, with a felted lining of horse-hair. The bird is an early breeder, the nest often being completed by the end of February or early in March, but the eggs, five or six in number, and of a pale reddish-buff colour, sometimes nearly white with red spots, are not, as a rule, laid till the end of March or beginning of April. The young are clad in a uniformly mottled greyish-green plumage, which, however, is soon moulted, and they then become like their parents. Several broods are hatched in the course of the season.

The sexes are practically alike and have the upper parts olive brown; frontal band, lore, chin, throat, and upper breast reddish-orange, bordered on the throat and breast with bluish-grey; flanks brown; rest of under parts white. Length 5·75 in.; wing 3 in.

Adult (right)   ROBIN (*Erithacus rubecula*)   Young (left)

12"

NIGHTINGALE (*Daulias luscinia*)

NIGHTINGALE

Daulias luscinia (Linnæus)

THIS migrant winters in Africa. On his arrival in Great Britain, about the third week in April, he pours out his ecstasy in glorious song. To attempt to describe that song is out of the question; loud and clear with full-toned deep liquid notes, now rising with impassioned fervour and then suddenly stopping, he recommences after a telling pause with a low, plaintive cry. There is no mistaking it when heard; it is the trained voice breathing soul and fire with every note.

A nesting site is chosen on the ground in some thicket, and a delicate cup is formed of dead leaves loosely laid together, with a lining of horse hair and other finer materials. The four to six eggs are olive-brown, rarely greenish-blue. The hen alone sits. Small woods and coppices are the situations most popular with these birds, especially narrow strips of woodland bordering fields, to which they often make excursions in search of food. This consists entirely of spiders and insects, flies being the main item.

The plumage above is warm brown, passing to reddish-brown on the tail and tail coverts; under parts greyish-white, buffish on the flanks and breast. The young have light centres to the feathers of the upper parts and are indistinctly barred on the breast. Length 6·5 in.; wing 3·35 in.

In Britain this bird has a very restricted range, being known only to the south-east of a line from the Humber to the Severn. It is sometimes heard in Shropshire and South Wales, and occasionally in Devonshire where it has been known to nest in rare instances.

WHITETHROAT. *Sylvia cinerea (Bechstein)*

QUIET and unobtrusive in colouring, and retiring in habit, this common summer visitor is often barely noticed. Early in April the Whitethroats begin to arrive after their winter sojourn in South Africa, and from then to the end of the month they populate our hedgerows in increasing numbers. When he first arrives, the bird may be seen sitting on some prominent twig, or on telegraph wires, trilling his short but pleasing song which is a mere medley of notes put together without apparent order or meaning. Anon he will drop from his perch into the hedge, throwing up his tail as he does so, and will rapidly wend his way by means of short leaps from twig to twig, exhibiting what seems like a creeping motion which has given rise to his local name, "Nettle-creeper." He is sometimes known as the Greater Whitethroat.

The nest, a delicate structure built low in some bush, or in a clump of nettles on the outside of the hedge, is composed of grass and bents lightly interwoven and lined with a few horse hairs. It looks very fragile. The eggs, four to six in number, are of a yellowish-olive colour, blotched with purplish-blue, especially at the larger end. The bird feeds on flies, caterpillars and insects generally. When the best of the summer is past they go to the shores of the Mediterranean and to Africa.

The male has the head and neck dark grey, mantle and wings brown with broad rufous edges to the secondaries. Tail feathers brown, except the outer pair that are white and the next pair that are tipped with white. Under parts white, fading to pale vinous on the breast and flanks. The female has the head brown, and is duller in colour. Length 5·5 in.; wing 2·8 in.

Common throughout Britain, except the extreme north of Scotland.

WHITETHROAT (*Sylvia cinerea*)

Female (above) BLACKCAP (*Sylvia atricapilla*) Male (below)

BLACKCAP

Sylvia atricapilla (Linnæus)

A FEW Blackcaps sometimes winter in Devon, but the bird is really migrant. Its winter quarters are mainly in Africa. We gladly welcome the little fellow when he makes his appearance in Britain about the middle of April. He is not often seen, for, like all his tribe, he haunts woods and coppices, keeping low down in their leafy shade, and hopping along quietly from branch to branch as we approach. Those who have not heard the song of the Nightingale suggest that his song is little inferior to that of the prince of avian songsters; but it is not only different, it lacks the passion and tone so marked in the song of the Nightingale.

The nest is built in low hedges, among nettles and at the base of bushes. It is a slight structure made of dry grass lightly woven and lined with a little horsehair. The four to six eggs are variable, being usually of a dirty creamish colour, blotched and spotted with darker brown, or sometimes of a reddish tint with dark-red spots.

The food consists almost entirely of insects, and it is on this diet that the young are reared, but as fruit ripens in the hedges or our gardens a large toll is taken, especially of currants and raspberries.

The adult male has the head black and the rest of the upper parts ash-brown. Chin greyish-white; throat, breast, and flanks ash-grey; belly white. Bill horn colour: legs leaden. The female has the top of the head reddish-brown and the young at first resemble her. The males assume their black head in their first autumn: sometimes the cap shows a reddish tinge. Length 5·75 in.; wing 2·75 in. Fairly common in England and Wales: more local in Scotland and Ireland.

GOLDEN-CRESTED WREN
Regulus cristatus (*K. L. Koch*)

THE smallest British bird. Resident. Though not often seen it abounds wherever a fir plantation is to be found. It flits about branches of conifers in restless search of small insects. It has hardly any song; the call-note is a feeble but penetrating high-pitched squeak often heard when the bird is invisible. The nest, a neat and beautiful structure, is deep and cup-shaped, the outside being as well finished as the interior. It is suspended from the end of a bough of some non-deciduous tree, being firmly secured to the small lateral twigs. It is composed of moss, leaves and fir needles woven with the aid of wool and cobwebs into a compact felted mass, the interior being lined with wool and a profusion of feathers. Six to ten eggs; creamy-white, minutely and profusely dotted with reddish-brown.

General colour above yellowish olive-green. Forehead whitish, bordered on either side by a blackish streak. Crown of head and crest bright lemon-yellow, becoming deep reddish-orange behind. Wings brown with white tips to the secondaries and a black bar across the upper part. Median and greater wing coverts with white margins. Under parts greenish-buff. The female lacks the bright orange in the crest and the young bird has no crest. Length 3·6 in.; wing 2·1 in.

THE FIRECREST (*Regulus ignicapillus*, C. L. Brehm) is a rare wanderer to our southern counties during the winter months. It does not nest with us. It may be overlooked on account of its similarity to the Goldcrest from which it is distinguished at all ages by a yellow frontal streak that passes backwards over the eye, succeeded by a black line through the eye, while another black streak runs backwards from the nape.

FIRE-CRESTED WREN (*Regulus ignicapillus*)
GOLDEN-CRESTED WREN (*Regulus cristatus*)

CHIFFCHAFF (above)   WILLOW WREN (below)
(*Phylloscopus collybita*)   (*Phylloscopus trochilus*)

CHIFFCHAFF
Phylloscopus collybita (Vieillot)

A MIGRANT which winters on Mediterranean coasts: arrives in Britain end of March or early April. It announces its arrival and its name by its note, a cheery "chiff-chaff". If we wish to see him, we have to watch carefully, for as we approach he will leave his post high in some tree and hide in the undergrowth. The food consists of small flies, other insects and larvae captured mainly among the leaves and branches of trees. Nesting begins April-May, the nest being loosely placed in some bramble thicket or undergrowth in a wood. It is domed, loosely built of bents, moss and leaves, and warmly lined with feathers. The five to seven eggs are white, dotted and spotted with dark reddish-brown. The upper parts are olive-green; wing coverts, quills and tail feathers brown, edged with the same colour: under parts whitish. A pale yellowish streak above the eye. Sexes alike: the young slightly greener. Length 4·6 in.; wing 2·35 in. Local in Scotland.

WILLOW WREN
Phylloscopus trochilus (Linnæus)

MIGRANT, wintering in Africa and Persia. Arrives here in vast numbers in early April. Closely allied to the Chiffchaff and resembling it in general appearance. This hardy little wanderer ranges as far north as the birch woods extend. Feeds chiefly on insects. Nest similar in size, shape and materials to that of the Chiffchaff: a domed structure with side entrance usually placed very near and often right on the ground. Eggs white with pale rufous spots, much paler, less clean-cut and more numerous than on those of the Chiffchaff. The bird is rather larger, brighter in colour and has paler legs than the Chiffchaff. Length 4·9 in.; wing 2·7 in.

HEDGE ACCENTOR
Accentor modularis (Linnæus)

KNOWN as the Dunnock and misnamed Hedge Sparrow. A British resident, numerous except in the extreme north. Frequents gardens, hedges, shrubberies, etc. Does incalculable good in destroying numbers of noxious insects, and when winter comes and such food is scarce, consumes seeds of all kinds, thus helping to keep down weeds. Towards evening, or when suddenly alarmed, utters a shrill "iss", rather like a pencil being drawn across a slate: during the breeding season his song is very sweet and unobtrusive, a low warble.

The bird nests from March to July. The nest is a beautiful structure of moss strongly felted together and lined with horsehair on a foundation of twigs and leaves: it is perfectly circular in shape and somewhat deep. Four to six eggs of a beautiful clear blue are laid. Altogether, this little home is in its quiet way one of the most beautiful of our common natural objects. It is placed in hedges, evergreens, ivy, in a furze bush or, maybe, a pile of faggots.

The sexes are nearly alike, the head, nape, chin, throat and upper breast are slate-grey, rest of the upper parts rufous-brown, with darker streaks; flanks brown streaked with darker, belly white. The female is slightly duller. The young are brown, spotted with buff all over. Length 5·5 in.; wing 2·75 in.

HEDGE ACCENTOR (HEDGE SPARROW) (*Accentor modularis*)

LONG-TAILED TIT (*Acredula caudata*)

LONG-TAILED TIT

Acredula caudata (Linnæus)

A BRITISH resident. There must be few who have not noticed this charming little bird when walking in winter along a hedgerow. We are attracted by a high-pitched "zi-zit" as the bird darts from the hedge in front of us, and after a few yards of undulating flight settles again. The bird frequents woodland shrubberies, hedgerows, etc., feeding on insects and their larvae. Nesting starts in April, the nest being placed in an open hedgerow, in a hedge bordering a wood, or in some isolated bush or tree in the wood itself. It is an elaborate, wonderful and beautiful structure, a solid, thick-walled elliptical domed mass of felted moss completely covered externally with lichens, which are largely interwoven by means of cobwebs. The entrance is towards the upper end, and the interior is lined with horsehair and innumerable feathers, as many as seven hundred having been counted in a single nest. The eggs number eight to twelve, they have a white ground speckled with light red.

The sexes are alike. The forehead and crown are white, bordered by a dark stripe, which runs from the bill over the eye to join the black of the nape and back. Wings dark brown; scapulars and rump pinkish; tail feathers black, the three outer pairs broadly tipped and margined with white. Under parts dull white and tinged with pink on the flanks and belly. The young are duller. Length 5·5 in.; wing 2·4 in.

Common throughout our islands except in Scotland, where it is somewhat local.

GREAT TIT

Parus major (Linnæus)

ALSO known as Ox-eye. A common British resident, except in the extreme North. On a bright morning in winter, when the leafless branches of the trees bear white traces of the night frost, we shall not walk far before the rasping "che-chi, che-chi" of the little Saw-sharpener, as he is often called, breaks on our ears. We soon see him climbing about the branches of some wayside tree, never still, now hanging head downwards as he inspects a bud, seeking for the insect it may contain, or plucking some berry which he holds between his feet and with a few hammerings of his powerful little beak breaks open to secure the seed.

The bird feeds on insects, seeds, fruit, nuts, fat, etc. Woods and orchards are his chief haunts, but gardens are frequently visited, and if nest-boxes with small entrance holes be hung up on the trees round the house, he and his mate may often be induced to hatch and rear their family under our protection and observation.

The nesting site is always a hole in a wall or tree, or even a letter-box. The nest is a large accumulation of moss, the whole space being filled up level and a little cup-like hollow being sunk in part of it. From six to twelve eggs, white, with a few reddish-brown blotches. The hen bird sits very closely and pecks at any intruding hand.

The sexes are alike in plumage. The whole of the head, chin, throat, and a median line running down the breast are of a glossy blue-black; cheeks white; mantle yellowish-olive, prolonged forwards to end in a light spot on the nape; wing coverts and tail bluish-grey, quills darker. Length 5·75 in.; wing 2·85 in. The young somewhat paler than their parents.

GREAT TIT (*Parus major*)

NUTHATCH (*Sitta cæsia*)

NUTHATCH
Sitta cæsia (Wolf)

A BRITISH resident fairly well distributed over the woodland portions of our southern and midland counties, becoming rarer towards the north. In Scotland only observed in a few counties; not met with in Ireland. A very shy bird, but most interesting to observe as he runs up and down tree-trunks with extreme facility, assuming, as he does so, many graceful and curious positions. It seems immaterial whether he be going up, down, sideways, forwards or backwards, for in all positions he seems equally at home. He will be more often heard than seen, as the sharp, shrill note will betray his whereabouts, though by keeping on the far side of the tree he avoids being seen. Insects are largely eaten in summer, but seeds, berries, nuts and beechmast form his chief food. Nuts and seeds are taken to some convenient crevice in the bark and hammered with the sharp, hard bill until they are broken and the kernel can be pulled out and eaten.

The nest is made in a hole in a tree or wall, or more rarely in a bank: the entrance is generally plastered up with mud till only a small circular hole just large enough to admit the bird is left. The inside of the cavity is lined with a few leaves and scraps of bark. The eggs bear close resemblance to those of the Great Tit, but are usually rather larger: they have a white ground boldly marked with reddish-brown. Five to eight form the clutch.

The general colour of the upper parts is bluish-grey, but all tail feathers, except the central pair, are blackish, barred and tipped with white and grey. A black stripe runs through the eye from the base of the bill. Under parts pale rufous shading to chestnut on flanks and under tail coverts. Length 5·7 in.; wing 3·4 in. Female and young rather duller.

WREN

Troglodytes parvulus (*K. L. Koch*)

A BRITISH resident common over the country. Skulking as a rule in the thick hedge bottom, among undergrowth in woods, or in a tangle of brambles on a common, he will suddenly hop on to an outstanding spray, rattle off his little song, which has a volume disproportionate to his size, and then, with quick whirring beats of his wings dive into the undergrowth again a few yards off. Always bright and perky as he hops along, with his short tail held up at right angles to the body, he searches for any small seeds or insects he can find.

The nest is a beautiful domed structure, very closely concealed among the ivy on a wall or tree, or sometimes in a grassy bank or the side of a stack. It is composed of leaves, moss, bents, etc., so arranged and chosen as to harmonise well with its surroundings. The entrance is a narrow round hole: the interior is warmly lined with hair and feathers. Breeding begins in April. Several nests are generally built by each pair; one only is lined, the others being left quite rough inside. These so-called "cocks' nests" are used as roosting places, and if the eggs be destroyed they may be lined and used as the home for a second clutch. The eggs, from five up to twelve, are white, sparsely spotted with red.

The whole bird is of a uniform reddish-brown, rather lighter on the chin and throat, minutely barred with black. There is a dull white streak over each eye. Length 3·5 in.; wing 1·9 in. Female smaller and duller; the young less distinctly barred.

In winter our native stock of this bird receives considerable additions from the Continent.

COMMON WREN (*Troglodytes parvulus*)
Lower figure, St. Kilda variety

PIED WAGTAIL (*Motacilla lugubris*)

PIED WAGTAIL
Motacilla lugubris (Temminck)

A BRITISH resident found generally in our isles, but scarcer in the north. We hear his "chizzit, chizzit" uttered during his dipping flight across the field towards the ivy-clad wall. His engaging habit of see-sawing his tail, of bobbing his head as he walks, his nimble little runs and aerial evolutions render him very attractive. His fondness for bathing has won him the name of Polly Dishwasher. This charming bird haunts meadows, streamsides, farmyards and gardens.

The nest is built in holes, recesses in water banks, wood piles, quarries, etc. It is composed of grass and bents lined with hair, feathers, etc. From four to six eggs are laid: they are white or greyish with greyish-brown spots. When the young leave the nest they are almost immediately taken into the grass fields where the flies, attracted by the feeding cattle, offer them an easy livelihood. Spiders, insects and their larvae form the principal diet, but seeds are also eaten.

In winter the sexes are alike, and grey in general colour with dark wings and tail (except the two outer feathers, which are white). The inner secondaries are also broadly edged with white. Under parts white. In summer, the chin and back are black, the forehead and a stripe across the face being white. Length 7·3 in.; wing 3·5 in. The young bird resembles the adult in winter, but the white portions, especially on the throat and breast, are tinged with yellowish and the breast is slightly spotted.

TREE PIPIT. *Anthus trivialis (Linnæus)*

A MIGRANT which winters in Africa and arrives here in April. Fairly common in England and Scotland, but becomes scarcer in the north. It may be heard singing its pretty little song near the outskirts of woods, or in fields bordered by trees. Its food, consisting almost entirely of insects, is generally sought on the ground. The nest is made in the middle of a field, or preferably in some bank or railway cutting: it is composed of roots and bents with a little moss and lined with finer bents and hair. The four to six eggs are variable; commonly greenish-white with bold blurred markings of dark brown at the larger end. In appearance the bird somewhat resembles a lark. Upper parts sandy brown with dark brown streaks; wing coverts darker, the median ones with pale edgings. Chin white, breast and flanks buff with darker markings: rest of under parts white. Tail feathers dark brown, except the two outer pairs which show some white. Sexes alike. Length 6 in.; wing 3·3 in.

MEADOW PIPIT. *Anthus pratensis (Linnæus)*

MOSTLY resident in Britain. Common. Haunts bleak and dreary moorlands, or wide wind-swept marshes and water meadows at all seasons. Feeds on insects and larvae, spiders, worms and small seeds. Nest made on the ground and concealed under a tussock: composed of grass and bents lined with finer grass and hair. Four to six eggs of a uniform brownish-grey colour, frequently mottled or clouded with a darker shade. Breeds May-June. The adult bird is olive-brown above, each feather having a darker centre, except on the rump and upper tail coverts: wing coverts margined with white. A narrow white eye-stripe. Under parts buffish-white streaked with brown on throat, breast and flanks. Sexes alike. Length 5·75 in.; wing 3·1 in.

TREE PIPIT (*Anthus trivialis*) (left)   MEADOW PIPIT (*Anthus pratensis*) (right)

36

RED-BACKED SHRIKE (*Lanius collurio*)
Adult male, female, and young

RED-BACKED SHRIKE
Lanius collurio (Linnæus)

Migrant wintering in Africa, and arriving in Britain at the end of April or in early May. Fairly common in our southern and south-eastern counties and in Wales during the summer months. Appears irregularly in northern counties. Bold and pugnacious, he sits on the top of some hawthorn hedge, dashing down from his point of observation on some mouse, bird or lizard as large as himself. After a tussle the hapless victim is carried off and impaled on a thorn near its captor's nest, to be eaten at a future time: it is these larders of impaled victims that have earned for him the name of Butcher Bird. Beetles and insects of all kinds are included in his menu, and half-fledged birds are considered a great delicacy.

The nest, built about June, is a large and loose structure of twigs, roots and moss; it is lined with hair and wool and placed about eight or ten feet from the ground in a thick hawthorn hedge. The four to six eggs are usually of a pale green colour, with a zone or band of olive-brown mottlings round the larger end.

The Shrike has no song, but makes a variety of harsh noises and chucklings as it sits on its post of vantage, bending down and flirting his tail at the same time. The call-note is a harsh "chack".

The adult male has the crown, nape and upper tail coverts grey; frontal band, lores, and ear coverts black; back chestnut; tail feathers black, all except the central pair with white bases; under parts rose-buff. The female has the upper parts brown, mantle rufous, with small narrow black crescentic bars on the feathers; under parts greyish-white barred like the mantle. The young bird resembles the female, but is more barred. Length 7 in.; wing 3·7 in.

SAND-MARTIN

Cotile riparia (Linnæus)

MIGRANT. Winters in Africa or India. Arrives in Britain early in
April before the Swallow. The smallest and dullest of the Swallow
tribe. At first he is generally seen in the neighbourhood of water,
but he gradually spreads over the country and eventually assembles
in sand-pits or gravel banks where he makes his home. Though
not attaching himself to the dwellings of man, like the Swallow
or House-Martin, he is a gregarious bird and breeds in colonies
which are in some places very large. The birds nest in tunnels
which they excavate for themselves in the perpendicular face of a
sand-pit. These tunnels are straight and narrow, with a slightly
enlarged chamber at the end. Their length varies from eighteen
inches to three feet, and the different passages occasionally meet
and may be used in common by two pairs. A slight lining of bents
and feathers are added and the four to six eggs are pure white and
somewhat pear-shaped. When the breeding season is over the
birds scatter through the country, keeping mainly to the courses
of large rivers, and by the end of September almost all have de-
parted to other climes.

The sexes are alike and have the upper parts brown. The under
parts are white, with the exception of a brown pectoral band. There
is a small tuft of buff-coloured feathers above the hind toe. In the
young the feathers of the back have pale margins. Length 4·8 in.;
wing 4 in.

Adult (right) SAND-MARTIN (*Cotile riparia*) Young (left)

40

Male (below)　　　　GREENFINCH (*Ligurinus chloris*)　　　　Female (above)

GREENFINCH

Ligurinus chloris (Linnæus)

RESIDENT in Britain. Abundant except in the far north. Were it not so common this bird would be appreciated as one of our prettiest songsters, and it is by no means unattractive in plumage. The winter is spent in company with other Finches and Buntings in the fields or stackyards, where it feeds on grain and other seeds. It does its share in despoiling the farmer, but pays some compensation by destroying numerous weeds.

Towards the end of April the Greenfinch constructs a somewhat untidy nest of twigs, rootlets, and moss, lined with grass, hair, and feathers. The nest is usually placed at a moderate height in a hedge, tree or shrub, or more rarely among ivy against a wall. The four to six eggs are large for the size of the bird: very pale blue, spotted, especially towards the larger end, with pale rust-red spots.

During the summer large numbers of grubs and caterpillars are consumed. The young are fed by regurgitation. The call-note is a long drawn-out "tsweer", and is uttered with monotonous frequency during the spring and summer months. But the bird has also a pretty warbling song full of little trills and modulations.

The male has the upper parts olive-green, rather yellower on the rump and forehead. There is a golden-yellow eye-stripe. Wing feathers dark brown with bright yellow outer margins. Tail feathers, except central pair, which are black, yellow at base, with black tips. Under parts greenish-yellow, rather darker on the flanks. Females much duller than males and very brown on upper parts in winter. Young yellowish-brown, streaked on breast with darker brown. Males do not assume full plumage till their second year. Length 6 in.; wing 3·5 in.

GOLDFINCH

Carduelis elegans (Stephens)

BRITISH resident, fairly generally distributed. Moves over the country in winter feeding on seeds and berries. Haunts commons, plantations, orchards, gardens, etc. Flocks are seen about thistles on waste lands in autumn. As we approach to get a closer view, first one and then another will rise and in undulating flight move on to another clump and call his companions to a fresh hunting-ground with his little "ti-whit." His bright colours and the ease with which he adapts himself to cage life have led to a diminution of his numbers, and, in addition, the more scientific methods of farming have restricted his feeding grounds. But the bird is now legally protected and he is increasing in numbers.

Nesting begins in May. The nest is built in fruit trees, sometimes in shrubs and thorn hedges: it is an open cup-shaped nest of moss, bents and small twigs, often covered on the outside with lichen so as to make it blend better with its surroundings. The lining is chiefly of hair and thistledown. The four or five eggs are blue, spotted and streaked, especially at their larger ends, with reddish-brown. The young are at first fed by the regurgitation of half-digested food from the crops of their parents and at this time many insects are eaten.

The Goldfinch, in its gay colouring, is so well and generally known that detailed description is hardly necessary. The female may be distinguished from the male by her more slender bill and brownish shoulders. In the adult male the shoulders are jet black, but young males sometimes show traces of brown. The young, known as "grey pates", are greyish-brown on the upper parts and lack the characteristic markings on the head. Length 5 in.; wing 3 in.

GOLDFINCH (*Carduelis elegans*)

Male (left)   Female (centre)   Young (right)

TREE-SPARROW (*Passer montanus*)

TREE-SPARROW

Passer montanus (Linnæus)

BRITISH resident. Although so closely allied to the ubiquitous House Sparrow, the Tree-Sparrow is a bird of quite different temperament and habit. It is worthy to be considered among our bird friends. It is a rather local and scarce bird, but even in places where it is common it is so shy that it is hardly ever seen, and in consequence it is considered much rarer than it really is. It shuns the habitations of man. It is partial to trees, seeking its food there as well as on the ground. In summer its food consists chiefly of insects, grubs and spiders: in winter seeds and berries are eaten. The notes closely resemble those of the House Sparrow, but are slightly more musical.

Holes in pollard willows or in some hedgerow tree are used for nesting. The hole accommodates a substantial nest of grass abundantly lined with feathers. Four to six eggs form the clutch: these are greyish in ground colour, delicately but thickly mottled with brown, and it is an almost invariable rule that one egg of the clutch should be conspicuously lighter than the others.

The adult has the crown and nape dark chestnut and this coloration marks it off from the House Sparrow, which has a slate-grey crown and nape. The rest of the upper parts are chestnut with darker centres to the feathers; upper and lower wing coverts tipped with white and forming two distinct bands. Cheeks white with a triangular black patch in the centre. Chin and throat black; rest of under parts greyish-white passing to brown in the flanks. Length 5·6 in.; wing 2·75 in. Sexes alike in plumage. Young similar to parents, but duller.

CHAFFINCH

Fringilla cœlebs (*Linnæus*)

RESIDENT and generally distributed in Britain. Often called "Pink";
known in Scotland as the Shilfa. Who does not know the Chaffinch
with his bright "pink-pink" and perky walk, as he goes down the
garden in front of us, or flies into the nearest shelter, showing off
the white bars on his wings as he does so. No matter how severe
the winter or how hot the summer, he is always with us, a constant
visitor to our gardens, and when we go into the woods and fields
we find him equally at home there. The bird is chiefly insectivorous
in summer: in winter it eats seeds and grain.

Nesting begins in April. The site chosen is variable—the fork of
some giant tree or against the trunk of a hedgerow elm supported
by a lateral shoot are the places most frequently used, but it is
often situated in a hedge, and sometimes in the ivy against a wall.
The nest itself is a beautiful mass of moss, grass and wool carefully
felted together with cobwebs and thickly lined with hair, lichens
being often added on the outside to make it blend better with the
surroundings. Eggs four to six, greenish-blue, spotted and clouded
with deep reddish-brown, but occasionally the markings are absent.

The male has the crown and nape bluish-grey; back reddish-
brown; rump greenish; upper wing coverts black tipped with
white and forming two conspicuous bars. Wing and tail feathers
black, the former edged with yellowish-white, and the two outermost pairs of the latter spotted with white; cheeks and under parts
reddish-brown. Bill horn-coloured in winter, deep lead-grey in
summer. Legs dark brown. The female is of various shades of
yellowish-brown, but the white wing bars are conspicuous. The
young at first resemble the female. Length 6 in.; wing 3·4 in.

CHAFFINCH (*Fringilla cœlebs*)

48

Male (above)   LINNET (*Linota cannabina*)   Female (below)

LINNET

Linota cannabina (*Linnæus*)

BRITISH resident. Fairly common in most parts of Britain except in mountain areas. Almost any kind of country suits him—hedges near open and cultivated land, furze-clad commons, or fields. May be seen in winter in small parties of from eight to ten flying from place to place, with cheery twittering, or, in severe weather in flocks of several hundreds. The food consists of seeds and berries, though insects are largely eaten during the summer months.

Nesting takes place from April to June and the nest is located in a bush or hedge at no great distance from the ground: it is a compact structure of grass and bents bound together with a little moss and wool, and lined with hair, wool, and feathers. The four to six eggs are of a delicate pale blue blotched with reddish-brown spots.

The song of this bird is a kind of continuous chuckling which is often delivered whilst on the wing. During the courting season the male indulges in a pretty love flight; he rises some distance in the air and then slowly descends with rapid flutterings of his wings and out-spread tail, singing at the same time with all his might.

The upper parts in the male are brownish, greyer on the nape and more rufous on the mantle. Wing and tail feathers black with white margins. Crown of head and breast deep crimson; flanks brown; belly white. Length 5·5 in.; wing 3·15 in. In winter the red on the crown and breast is deep brown and the feathers of those parts have broad yellowish margins. The female resembles the male on the upper parts, but the mantle is duller and the white of the primaries is less in extent. Under parts yellowish-brown streaked with dark brown: head also streaked with brown. Young resemble the female, but paler.

4

BULLFINCH
Pyrrhula Europæa (Vieillot)

BRITISH resident. Occurs in fair numbers in most parts of the country, but is local in Scotland. Haunts woods, coppices, thick hedgerows and gardens. Rather a skulking species, but may be recognised when on the wing by its white rump. The call-note is a rather plaintive "whee-ou". The bird is easily attracted by imitating its call. Possibly it pairs for life: it is generally seen in pairs; even in winter the male shows affection for his mate by keeping close to her and feeding her. The song is a feeble medley of soft flute-like notes, and is usually accompanied by a side-to-side motion of the tail and body.

The species nests from May to July. The nest is a shallow plat-form of twigs placed three or four feet from the ground in a thick bush or hedge; it is lined with fine rootlets. The four to six eggs are greenish-blue spotted and streaked round the larger end with black or purplish-lilac. The young are fed by regurgitation. Insects form a big proportion of the parents' food during the summer. In autumn, berries, especially those of the privet, are consumed, but in winter the dietary is extended to all kinds of seeds. In spring attention is turned to young buds, especially those of fruit-trees.

The male has the whole of the head a glossy blue-black; mantle brownish-grey. Larger wing coverts black tipped with whitish to form a conspicuous bar. Primaries brown; secondaries and tail glossy black; rump white. The whole of the under parts bright brick-red turning to white on the vent. Female duller, with under parts a uniform brown. The young resemble the hen but lack the black crown. Length 6 in.; wing 3·25 in.

Male (right)   BULLFINCH (*Pyrrhula europæa*)   Female (left)

YELLOW BUNTING

Emberiza citrinella (*Linnæus*)

KNOWN as Yellow Hammer and in Scotland as Yellow Yite. A common British resident. In spring and early summer may be seen sitting on the topmost spray of a hedge and repeating with monotonous frequency its little song, "A little bit of bread and no cheese". Frequents hedges, lanes, farmyards, and more open country. The bird is essentially a seed-eater, destroying in countless numbers the seeds of various weeds amongst cultivated crops. In summer insects are largely eaten.

Nesting begins in April. The nest is built near ground amongst growth at the base of a bush or hedgerow; sometimes actually on the ground. It is a neat structure of grass, roots and moss woven together and lined with horsehair. Eggs from three to five; purplish-white, scribbled, streaked and veined with purplish-red.

In autumn, young and old visit standing crops in family parties, and they pass the winter seeking their food on the ground in stubbles and fallows or visiting the stack-yards for the fallen grain.

The male has head, throat and under parts bright yellow, spotted or streaked, except on the throat, with dark brown. Mantle yellowish-brown with darker streaks. Rump reddish-brown. Wings brown with broad, deep rufous edgings to the secondaries and wing coverts. Tail feathers dark brown with white spots near the tip of the inner web of the two outer pairs. The female resembles the male, but is much duller and darker in colour. The young are pale brown all over, lighter on the under parts and more rufous on the back, each feather having a dark central stripe. Length 6·5 in.; wing 3·25 in.

STARLING

Sturnus vulgaris (Linnæus)

RESIDENT in Britain and very common. Tame, confiding, and an excellent mimic, he is welcome wherever found. Frequents gardens, fields, etc. In his fanciful way, David Grayson describes parties of this bird grubbing on the lawn as behaving like old ladies at a tea-party. In autumn the species congregates in vast flocks whose numbers reach thousands: these flocks go through their aerial evolutions, now drawing close together in a compact mass, or spreading out in wedge-shaped formation, rising and falling as though they were one.

Any hole in a tree or wall, the roof of a house, drain-pipes, church towers, or cliffs suit this species for a nesting-site. An untidy mass of straw, grass, and rubbish is collected to form a nest, and a few feathers, or some wool, are added as lining. The four to six eggs are of a uniform pale blue.

The bird feeds chiefly on insects, worms and slugs, which are sought for in damp meadows, pasture-lands and lawns. It walks in a curious deliberate way, and on seeing a likely worm casting it pushes in its closed beak, and after drawing it back with open mandibles, the hole, thus enlarged, is examined for its contents. Also partial to sheep runs, settling on the sheep's back and relieving it of many ticks and other parasites.

Sexes practically alike and in winter the whole of the plumage is glossy black with metallic reflections. The feathers of the upper parts are tipped with buff and those of the under parts with white. In summer almost all the spots on the under parts are lost as well as a large proportion of those on the back. Bill lemon-yellow in summer, blackish in winter. Young greyish-brown all over, rather lighter on chin and under parts. Length 8·5 in.; wing 5·2 in.

Adult (right)   STARLING (*Sturnus vulgaris*)   Young (left)

JAY (*Garrulus glandarius*)

JAY
Garrulus glandarius (*Linnæus*)

BRITISH resident. Frequents woodlands. Not common in Scotland. Considering the ruthless war waged on this unfortunate species by every gamekeeper throughout the country, it is remarkable that we can still hear his harsh scream in most of our woods. He is very wary and cautious, and spends most of his time on the tops of trees, except when actually feeding, flying off with many protestations to another part of the wood on the least sign of danger. His supposed great sin is the destruction of Pheasants' eggs, though it is doubtful if his depredations are sufficiently extensive to warrant his wholesale slaughter. Noisy and active as he is during the winter, in spring he becomes exceptionally quiet, and only when his nest is approached does he give any indication of his presence in the neighbourhood.

The nest, from April to May, is generally placed some ten feet from the ground in the fork of a tender sapling and is made entirely of twigs and lined with fine roots. It is open and cup-shaped, and the four to six eggs, small for the size of the bird, are pale green, very thickly mottled with olive-brown with, generally, a narrow black irregular line at the larger end. The young are fed chiefly on insects, spiders and grubs, but the species is practically omnivorous. Large numbers of berries are eaten in winter.

The general colour of the nape, mantle and under parts is vinous-brown. Crown of the head whitish, streaked with black; malar stripe black. Chin, rump and under tail coverts white; tail and primaries black, the latter with white outer margins. Secondaries black, the outermost five with white bases. Wing coverts barred white, black and blue. The sexes and young alike in plumage. Length 14·25 in.; wing 7·2 in.

MAGPIE

Pica rustica (Scopoli)

BRITISH resident. Fairly common where it is not persecuted, for this is another species against which every man's hand in this country is raised. It frequents large open fields dotted with bushes and trees. Bold and omnivorous, it finds little difficulty in procuring a livelihood, and if it settles in the neighbourhood of a poultry or game farm it does no little damage thereto. On the other hand, it destroys countless worms, slugs, mice, and even young rats, so that by no means is the bird wholly mischievous. A fine showy bird, it is a pleasure to see him as he flies with rapid beats of his short wings across some field, rattling out his cheery chatter as he goes.

The nest, usually built in April, is a huge domed structure substantially made of twigs, those with sharp spikes or thorns being used for preference. It is placed high in trees, and in bushes and hedges. Inside, a deep cup is made of mud, and inside this again is placed a thick lining of grass. The egg clutch may number from five to eight: the eggs are of a bluish colour irregularly dotted, mottled, or splashed with olive-brown. The bird is strictly resident, rarely wandering from its accustomed haunts, and frequently going about in pairs.

The whole bird is glossy black with bluish and green reflections, except for the scapulars and belly, which are white. The rump is greyish. Length, including tail, 18 in.; tail 10 in.; wing 7·75 in. The sexes and young are all much alike in plumage.

59

MAGPIE (*Pica rustica*)

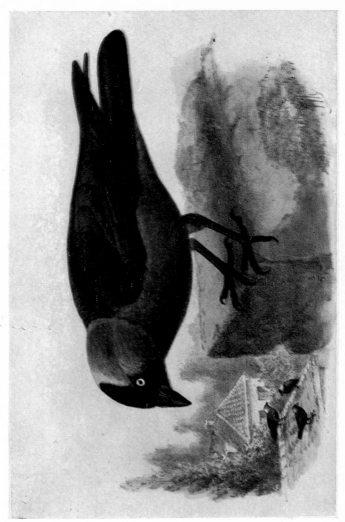

JACKDAW (*Corvus monedula*)

JACKDAW

Corvus monedula (*Linnæus*)

A BRITISH resident, abundant and gregarious in most parts of the country. In winter associates with flocks of rooks in open pastures and arable land. A noisy bird, and its call-note "che-ak" will generally warn us of its presence. It is found in all kinds of situations and localities, being equally at home in the wild open country, along the coast, rocky or alluvial, or on arable land, in well-timbered districts, and even in the middle of our busy cities; but although abundant in some towns, it is remarkable that in others equally suitable it is hardly ever found. Practically omnivorous, he experiences no difficulty in procuring a living wherever he may be, but will usually be found associated with Rooks or Starlings on the pastures, often perching on the backs of sheep to rid them of the parasites with which they are infected.

Holes in trees, walls, or ruins, church towers, chimneys, or cavities in rocks provide suitable nesting-sites. In April a rough nest is built of sticks, lined with abundance of fur, rabbit flock, wool and any other soft material. The four to six eggs are pale blue, with large distinct spots of olive-brown.

The sexes are practically indistinguishable, and are of a glossy purplish-black on the head and back, and of a somewhat duller greyish-black below. The occipital region, nape, and sides of the neck are clear grey, forming a sort of collar. The young birds are duller and lack the grey collar, which is only partially assumed in the first year. Length 13 in.; wing 9·25 in.

ROOK

Corvus frugilegus (Linnæus)

A BRITISH resident, common in favoured localities. Frequents fields, woods, seashore, etc. Year after year the birds return to the same clump of trees, on the tops of which they build a fairly substantial nest of sticks, with an inner foundation of mud which is in turn warmly lined with roots, straw, and fine grass. The sites chosen for their homes are frequently near human habitations or on clumps of trees near a highway, sometimes they may choose pollards, but as a rule the nests are never less than twenty feet from the ground. The eggs are bluish, with olive-brown spots and blotches. The breeding season is from March to May.

These birds are rather capricious and will occasionally, even in the nesting season, desert the colony. As soon as the young can fly, towards the middle or end of May, the rookery is deserted: old and young keep together and wander about the fields and arable land, digging deeply with their powerful bills in search of larvae and grubs, and destroying countless numbers of wire worms. In this country the species does not migrate to any extent; certain plantations are used as regular roosting-places, and as evening draws on in the winter months, long strings of the birds may be seen slowly flying in their heavy manner to their nightly shelter.

From continual digging the feather follicles round the base of the bill become destroyed, leaving a patch of whitish bare skin: this is characteristic of adult birds. In young individuals, however, the feathers extend to the base of the bill and do not appear to be lost till during the second autumn moult. The sexes are alike—a uniform deep and glossy purplish-blue. The young resemble their parents, but are duller. Length 19 in.; wing 12·65 in.

63

Adult (right)   ROOK (*Corvus frugilegus*)   Young (left)

SKYLARK

Alauda arvensis (*Linnæus*)

A BRITISH resident and abundant throughout the country. Its favoured haunts are pasture lands, commons, downs and moors. A bird of the open spaces. Its song during its high, perpendicular flight is recognised by all.

The neat nest of bents and dry grass lined with finer materials is placed in a hollow on the ground in the middle of an open field. Two or three broods are reared from April to July. There are four or five eggs, greyish-white, clouded and thickly mottled with dark brown and grey.

The food is of a very varied nature and nothing comes amiss. The young are fed exclusively on insects, but after leaving the nest they spend their time eagerly feeding on seeds, berries, or anything that comes their way. As summer wanes, the birds collect in large flocks and seek the stubble fields, where the scattered grain gives them abundant nourishment, and on which they become very fat. In October they become restless, and many wander to the coast, and thence to other countries, their place being taken by others from more northerly climes.

The adult has the general plumage of a warm brownish tint, mottled and streaked with a darker shade. There is a light coloured superciliary streak. Chin, throat, upper breast and flanks brownish-buff streaked with brown; rest of under parts yellowish-white. The sexes are alike in plumage, but the female is rather smaller. The young have the chin and throat unspotted, and have pale edgings to the feathers of the upper parts. Length about 7 in.; wing (of male) 4 to 5 in.

SWIFT

Cypselus apus (Linnæus)

SOMETIMES called Screech Martin or Black Swallow. A migrant which winters in Africa. One of the last of the summer birds to arrive, May being generally well advanced before we hear its harsh yet pleasant scream of "swee ree" as it swerves in rapid flight round the cottage or belfry which is to form its summer home. The most aerial of all our native birds, and never seen to settle except when entering the hole under the eaves where it nests, and, in fact, owing to the length of its wing and shortness of its legs, it cannot raise itself from a level surface should it once settle.

Gregarious in its habits, it returns yearly to the same place and, entering through a hole or crevice under the eaves, nests there in security. Swifts as a family differ from other birds in using a sticky, mucous saliva with which to bind together rough bits of straw, cobwebs, feathers, etc., which form their nest. It does not often collect material, but makes use of the accumulation of rubbish usually found under roofs and, hollowing out a shallow depression, cements it into a permanent cup. The eggs, two or three in number, are dull white and oblong.

Swifts occasionally perform curious aerial evolutions on warm summer nights. As darkness approaches they become restless, screaming round tower or belfry as they dash by in wide circles; gradually they rise higher and higher till they become mere specks.

The sexes and young are alike in plumage; a uniformly dark sooty brown, the chin and throat being dull white. Tail short and slightly forked; wings long and narrow. The feet are extremely feeble, the four toes all directed forward and having sharp, recurved nails which enable them to cling to perpendicular surfaces. Length 6·5 in.; wing 6·8 in.

COMMON SWIFT (*Cypselus apus*)

68

GREATER SPOTTED WOODPECKER (*Dendrocopus major*)

Male (right)   Female (centre)   Young (left)

GREATER SPOTTED WOODPECKER
Dendrocopus major (Linnæus)

RESIDENT in Britain. Although it can nowhere be called abundant, this species is widely distributed in well-wooded districts as far north as Durham, but in Scotland it is a scarce bird, only nesting sparingly in the south; and in Ireland it is almost unknown. A quiet and shy bird, it is rarely seen, keeping as it does to the higher branches of tall trees, and when possible keeping the trunk between it and any would-be observer. Feeds on insects, particularly beetles and ants.

Nesting occurs from May to June. The material of the nest is merely chips of wood at the bottom of a hole in a tree, the hole being excavated by the bird. Eggs usually five or six, creamy white, glossy.

The call-note is a sharp, short "chik", but it also makes a peculiar rattling sound by rapping its beak against a bough. This sound, which is often heard in early spring, has been supposed to be made only at that season, but it may also be heard, though less frequently, at other times of the year.

In winter the species is much given to wandering, and every autumn our local birds receive further additions from Scandinavia.

The upper parts of the male are chiefly black; the forehead, cheeks, ear coverts, and scapulars are white; nape crimson; wing feathers black, barred with white on the outer webs; under parts whitish; vent crimson. The female lacks the red on the head, but the young of both sexes have the crown red. Length 9·4 in.; wing 5·5 in.

KINGFISHER
Alcedo ispida (*Linnæus*)

A RESIDENT generally observed in Great Britain in its favourite haunts, except in the north of Scotland and Ireland where it is rare. Its beauty creates a demand for its skin, but despite this the bird survives in our midst. As he darts with rapid flight down our streams he resembles a large, animated turquoise.

Having fixed on a favoured piece of water, the bird seldom wanders far afield, but may be seen at all times of the year, sitting on an overhanging bough, ever and anon dropping into the water to seize some passing fish. His prey captured, he returns to his perch and kills the struggling fish by knocking it against his stand; it is then swallowed head first, and the motionless watch is resumed. When streams are frozen the bird leaves his usual home for the seashore, but he remains there no longer than necessary. Like most bright-plumaged birds, he has no song with which to woo his mate, but at mating time they may be seen chasing each other up and down the stream, uttering a shrill and sharp call-note.

Nesting starts from March to April. A perpendicular wall in the bank of the stream is chosen and near the top of this a long low tunnel is excavated with the end widened to form a chamber. The nesting material consists of small regurgitated bones formed into a mass, and on this six or seven pure white, highly glossed eggs are laid.

Sexes practically alike in plumage. Top of the head, wings, and malar stripe dark greenish-blue, mottled with lighter; back and rump brilliant cobalt blue; tail dark blue. Under parts, lores, and ear coverts chestnut; throat whitish; bill black, orange at the base; legs deep red. Young bird duller, showing traces of greenish on the breast. Length 7·5 in.; wing 3 in.

KINGFISHER (*Alcedo ispida*)

Adult (below)   CUCKOO (*Cuculus canorus*)   Young (above)

CUCKOO

Cuculus canorus (Linnæus)

A MIGRANT. Winters in Central Africa and South India. The arrival of the Cuckoo, heralded by his well-known note, is eagerly awaited by every one who lives in the country. It is usually mid-April when his welcome note is generally heard. Common and well known in our islands, the bird occupies equally the wild open country, the enclosed arable land, or thickly wooded estates. It feeds on insects, especially caterpillars, those of the Tiger-moth being a favourite delicacy. The flight is direct and fairly rapid, the short wings and long tail giving the appearance of a Sparrow-Hawk, for which it is often taken by the smaller birds.

The bird is parasitic. It watches other birds when they are building, and as soon as the chosen nest contains a few eggs, it lays its own egg and deposits it in the nest, throwing out some of the rightful eggs. Having deposited its eggs one each in several nests, the mother Cuckoo takes no further interest in her progeny, leaving it to be nurtured by the foster parents. Early in August both sexes leave for their winter quarters. The eggs are extremely variable, small in proportion to the size of the bird: as a rule they are pale bluish or greenish in ground colour, with reddish spots and mottlings. Sometimes they very nearly resemble the eggs of their foster parents. When the young Cuckoo is hatched, he expels the other nestlings. The nests most favoured here are those of the Meadow Pipit, Pied Wagtail, Hedge Accentor, Sedge and Reed Warblers.

The male is clear greyish-ash on back and throat; tail feathers blackish with small white spots on the margin. Under parts whitish, with dark bars on the flanks. The young vary considerably, they are generally dark brown, more or less barred with rufous on the upper parts. Length 13 in.; wing 8·5 in.

TAWNY OWL
Syrnium aluco (Linnæus)

ALSO known as Brown or Wood Owl. Resident. A common inhabitant of the well-wooded parts of England, Wales and Scotland, though in the north of Scotland it becomes decidedly scarce and local. Not seen in Ireland.

The Tawny Owl nests early in March; it makes no proper nest, but places its eggs in a hollow tree, in crevices of cliffs or buildings, or in deserted nests of Rooks, Crows, or Hawks, or occasionally on ground at the base of a tree. The eggs are white and glossy, almost spherical.

The bird is extremely nocturnal in habit, very seldom appearing till quite dark. On very rare occasions it has been seen in broad daylight and then only under peculiar circumstances. It feeds on small mammals and birds; occasionally on insects and fish. It seldom pursues its prey in the open, but keeps mainly to glades and rides in the woods. Its hoot is a loud "hoo-hoo", and is repeated with frequency. This bird is never met with on migration: it rarely wanders from its birthplace.

The sexes are alike, except that the female is slightly larger. The general colour is usually of a warm tawny brown, mottled and streaked with darker shades of the same colour; the under parts are pale buffish-white, striped with dark brown. There are two phases of this species which are alike in markings, but in one the predominating tint is red and in the other grey. Length 15 in.; wing 10 in.

75

TAWNY OWL (*Syrnium aluco*)

Male (below)   KESTREL (*Falco tinnunculus*)   Female (abov

KESTREL

Falco tinnunculus (Linnæus)

ALSO known as the Windhover. May be seen on any fine day high in the air, remaining apparently motionless, but ever and anon keeping his position by a few rapid and quivering wing-beats. When his quarry is spotted, he swoops to the ground and seizes it. The bird is a British resident and is fairly common in spite of persecution. He feeds on mice and small rodents, occasionally small birds. Frequents moorlands, downs, commons, open fields, woods and cliffs.

The breeding season is from April to May. No nesting material is collected: the eggs are laid on ledges of cliffs, quarry faces, or ruins, or often the deserted nests of Crows or Magpies are occupied. From four to six eggs are laid; they are of a beautiful rich red colour in general appearance—on closer examination it is seen that they are of a yellowish-white ground colour obscured by various deep shades of red or brown. When the young are hatched they are thickly covered with pale greyish down. At first their parents tear their food for them and allow them to peck it from their beaks. Later it is passed to them whole and they tear it themselves. When the young are in the nest the parents hunt for prey away from home so as not to betray their offspring.

The adult male on the upper parts is of a deep chestnut, spotted or barred with black; under parts pale buff, striped with black. The head and nape are bluish-grey, as is also the tail, which has a sub-terminal black band and is tipped with white. The female is more barred on the back and has the head brown, striped with darker. The tail is rufous, barred with black and slightly tinged with grey. The young resemble the female. Length 14 in.; wing 9·5 in.

SHAG

Phalacrocorax graculus (Linnæus)

ALSO known as Green Cormorant on account of its green plumage. This bird is a British resident widely distributed round our coasts, especially near those rocky parts abounding in caves, on the ledges of which it breeds. It is a smaller and more local species than the Cormorant, to which it is closely related, and is never found breeding inland. In all other ways it is a counterpart of its larger congener and it is often confused with it by local fishermen. It is most common on the west coasts of England, Scotland, and Wales. It feeds on fish. During the breeding season it is rather noisy, the note being a harsh "kraik, kraik".

The nest is an untidy structure of sticks, seaweed and often straw. Where there are caves in which to nest, cliff ledges are occupied. The eggs number from three to five. They are blue, but the colour is often obscured by a chalky encrustation which gets stained by the damp nesting material. The breeding season is March to April. The nestlings are at first bare, but as they develop feathers they become brownish-green above, mottled with brown below.

The adult is of a uniform glossy bronze-green and wears for a short time in spring an upright and forwardly-directed crest. The tail has twelve tail feathers, and this forms an unmistakable character at all ages. The absence of the pale gular pouch will also enable the species to be recognised when on the wing. Length 27 in.; wing 10·75 in.

Adult in breeding dress   SHAG (*Phalacrocorax graculus*)   Young on sea

79

MALLARD OR WILD DUCK. *Anas boschas* (*Linnæus*)

THE commonest and most beautiful British Duck. Feeds chiefly by night on worms, aquatic insects, water weeds and grain. Prefers ditches overgrown with weeds or shallow ponds.

Nests March-May usually on the ground and at no great distance from water, but exceptionally has nested in trees, faggots, stacks, and other elevated places. A cup-shaped hollow is scraped out and this is warmly lined with down after incubation commences. From eight to fourteen eggs are laid; they are white with a greenish tinge and are always covered by the duck when she leaves her nest.

In its wild state the Mallard, as the male is called, is strictly monogamous, and during the whole period of incubation will remain near the nest, warning the female of approaching danger, and accompanying her when she comes off to feed. Once the young are hatched he retires to some secluded piece of water where he assumes a dull plumage, resembling that of the female. In this period he rarely shows himself in open water. He casts all his flight feathers at once and for a short time cannot fly. Within a fortnight he grows new feathers, and about September assumes his brilliant colours once more and emerges to join his comrades. In winter large flocks are formed which feed about marshes and the shore in evenings and retire to the water to rest at daybreak.

The male has a glossy green head and neck, the latter being circled by a narrow white ring; rump and tail coverts glossy greenish-black, the four central coverts upturned; chest and breast deep chestnut; rest of under parts pale grey, vermiculated with black; bill greenish-yellow; legs orange. The female is dark brown, the feathers having paler edgings. Young resemble female, but the males assume full dress by October. Length 23 in.; wing 11 in.

6

TUFTED DUCK

Fuligula cristata (Leach)

THE commonest of our Diving Ducks, nesting in increasing numbers near many inland waters throughout England, Scotland and Ireland. In winter, as is the case with most Ducks, large numbers arrive from abroad, and may be found in shallow bays, estuaries and inland waters in company with other species. It feeds mainly on vegetable matter, but also consumes molluscs, insects, etc. It makes very good eating after it has been in inland waters for some time.

The nest is usually made near water under bushes, among rushes and other herbage. It is composed of sedges, dried grass, etc., and lined with down. One brood is brought off about May. The eight to ten eggs are greenish-buff, and are said to hatch after about twenty-three days' incubation.

The adult has the crest, head and neck purplish-black; speculum white. Under parts, including the flanks, snow-white. Bill slate-grey; eye golden yellow; legs bluish. In the eclipse plumage it becomes much browner, somewhat resembling the female. The female is sooty brown above and greyish-brown below, and her crest is much shorter than that of the male. At the end of summer she becomes white round the base of the bill for two or three months, but individuals vary much in this respect. The young resemble the female, and have a whitish forehead. Length 17·25 in.; wing 8 in.

TUFTED DUCK (*Fuligula cristata*)

STOCK DOVE (*Columba œnas*)

STOCK DOVE
Columba œnas (Linnæus)

THE Stock Dove is rather smaller and considerably less common than the well-known Wood Pigeon which abounds in Britain and seems to be increasing. But the present species is by no means uncommon in England and has greatly increased of late years in Scotland. In Ireland it is still a rare and local species. The name "Stock Dove" is not due, as so many erroneously suppose, to its being the race from which our domestic pigeons spring, but to its habit of nesting in the stocks and boles of old timber. Such places, however, are by no means exclusively used, for it also nests in caves, on ledges of cliffs, and in rabbit-burrows. In other respects its habits do not differ materially from those of the Wood Pigeon. As a rule it goes about in pairs, and large flocks are never met with, even when the species is migrating from its more northerly breeding quarters.

Laying begins as early as March and may continue till October. There are two or three broods. In a burrow no nesting material may be used, but usually there is a loose arrangement of a few twigs, rootlets, etc. Eggs two, glossy white.

The head of this bird is bluish-grey, as also are the throat, wings and lower parts. Metallic reflections on portion of neck. Breast vinous, a spot of black on last two secondaries and some of wing coverts. Tail grey with black bars near end. The bill is yellow, red at its base. Feet red. Lacks the white spot on the neck which is a feature of the Wood Pigeon. Length 13·5 in.; wing 8·8 in. The note of this bird is a low cooing one: some observers describe it as a "grunting".

RED GROUSE
Lagopus scoticus (*Latham*)

RESIDENT in moorland areas of the North of England, Wales, Scotland and Ireland. Claimed to be an exclusively British bird. A strictly monogamous species, pairing early in the season, when his call-note, "go back, go back", may be heard. Generally nests from April to June, sometimes in March. One brood is hatched. The male waits on the female during incubation, warning her of the approach of danger with a sharp "kok, kok, kok". The nest is simply a scrape among the heather, no materials being added. Seven to twelve or more eggs are laid: they are very handsome, being of a pale ground colour, thickly and profusely marked with dark reddish-brown.

The food consists of various seeds and berries, together with the leaves and shoots of plants, and the tips of ling and heather; in autumn the harvest fields are visited. The young are fed on insects.

This species keeps, as a rule, in family parties, only packing together during severe weather in the less exposed places, but where they are much driven and shot they are often found in large flocks.

Specimens vary considerably in plumage. The male is dark brown, barred with reddish, and is often nearly black on the breast and whitish on the vent. The female is similarly coloured, but lighter. Length 16 in.; wing 8·4 in.

Male (left)   RED GROUSE (*Lagopus scoticus*)   Female (right)

PARTRIDGE (*Perdix cinerea*)

PARTRIDGE

Perdrix cinerea (*Latham*)

BRITISH resident. In England the Partridge is an exceedingly abundant bird, but in Scotland and Ireland, although well distributed, it is much more local. It is strictly monogamous, pairing very early in the year, but nesting operations are rarely commenced before the end of April or early in May. A truly ground bird, and a swift runner, but when forced to fly it makes a rapid flight with much whirring of wings for a distance, then skims the air and alights where it feels safe. In order to take attention from the nest or the young when approached, the parents often behave as if they have been injured. Sometimes two hens occupy the same nest. The Partridge chiefly inhabits open, cultivated districts, where it feeds on various seeds and grain. In summer insects are largely consumed and the young at first are fed on them exclusively. During the early autumn and winter the various families keep together, forming the well-known "coveys", but if the weather be severe these birds will "pack" in large flocks like Grouse.

The nest is a scrape in some hedge bottom, or on a grassy bank, or in a field. The eggs laid number from seven up to twenty: they are olive-brown.

In plumage, the male bird is grey on the neck and the front of the chest. In other parts it is variegated with grey and reddish-brown. There is a dark chestnut patch, horseshoe shaped, on the lower breast. The wing coverts are longitudinally striped with buff. The female is almost similar, but its wing coverts are barred, not striped. In the young birds the general tone of the plumage is paler, and the feathers have a median buff longitudinal stripe. Length 12·5 in.; wing 6 in.

MOOR-HEN

Gallinula chloropus (Linnæus)

MORE correctly known as the Water-hen. A British resident,
occurring wherever some water surrounded by cover is found, even
though it be a small ditch or pond. It has even penetrated into the
heart of London, and may be watched as it comes out to pick up
crumbs thrown by the passer-by, and then takes them back to her
young concealed in the rushes. The food consists of insects, worms,
slugs, aquatic vegetation and some grain. In some districts damage
is done to water-cress beds, the tender shoots being nipped off.
Truly a water bird, although it can run on the ground with ease.

In March or April several nests are partially built: these are
generally situated in clumps of sedge or rushes, but sometimes
under bushes or in trees some distance from the ground. In one of
the partially built structures the eggs will be laid, and when this
happens a considerable amount of material is added, and the higher
leaves of the surrounding plants are often bent over to afford con-
cealment. The nest is a rounded, well-compacted structure of dry
reeds and aquatic vegetation, with a lining of finer material. Seven
to nine eggs are laid, sometimes more: they are a buffish or reddish
yellow, spotted with reddish-brown. Both parents feed and tend the
young, and on the approach of danger safety is sought in diving.

Sexes much alike: upper parts dark olive-brown; head, neck and
under parts bluish-grey; the flank feathers streaked with white;
under tail coverts white. Bill bright red at the base, with yellow tip
in summer; dull olive-brown in autumn and early winter. Legs
greyish-yellow. The young have the chin white and under parts
greyish-brown: they are greyer on the back than the adults.
Length 13 in.; wing 6·75 in.

MOOR-HEN (*Gallinula chloropus*)

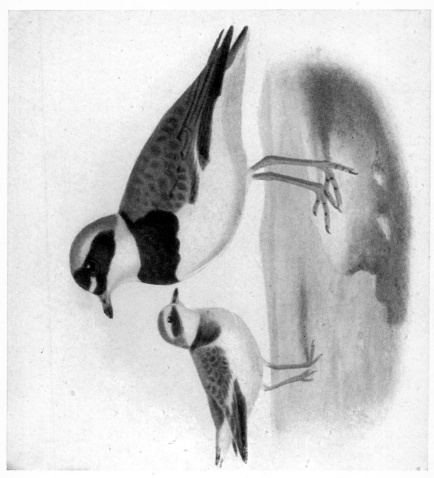

RINGED PLOVER

Ægialitis hiaticola (Linnæus)

BRITISH resident. Few people have walked along our shores without being attracted by the plaintive whistle of this delightful little bird. There is no month of the year when we cannot find it on our shores whatever be the weather. He is seen at his best in the breeding season. Walking along the shore, we see him running ahead: we sit down to watch him and he suddenly stops—then he runs to some stone slightly higher than its neighbours and stands up and watches us. His mate joins him and they stand together, now running a few yards, then turning to give us another look, bobbing their heads up and down. Finally, seeing that we do not go away, they both fly off: but in a minute or so one of them is back again, watching us from his old stand. The hen will be sitting on her eggs.

The nest is made on a beach, near high-water level. It is a mere scrape among the pebbles, sometimes unlined, but usually lined with bits of shells, small pebbles and possibly a few grasses. The four eggs are pear-shaped, laid with points to the centre of the clutch: they are yellowish or stone-colour with brownish-black spots, practically indistinguishable from the shingle among which they lie. The young are covered with thick down when hatched: as soon as they discard the shell they leave the nest and shortly begin to feed on flies, spiders and small insects to be found.

The sexes are alike in plumage. General colour above sandy brown: white beneath. Forehead white, succeeded by a black band; lores and band across chest black. Legs bright yellow; beak black, yellow at its base. The young resemble the adults, but lack the black band on the forehead. Legs olive-green. Length 7·75 in. Distributed along the shore and in some inland sandy places.

LAPWING

Vanellus vulgaris (Bechstein)

COMMONLY known as Peewit. British resident. Common. Frequents meadow-lands, arable land, sheep pastures, marshes, low hills and open country. A familiar bird with an unusually jerky flight, the wings making a noise like a fan as they beat the air. On ground a nimble runner. Feeds on worms, slugs, insects, etc.

Laying takes place in April. The nest is made in a hollow in the ground of a meadow, moor or marsh: it is a shallow platform of roots and bents placed in a "scrape". Four pear-shaped eggs are laid; ground colour variable, greenish-brown, olive-green, stone-colour, with deep brownish-black spots and blotches. When disturbed, in order that the eggs may not be located by the intruder, the female runs quietly along the ground before taking flight and the male distracts attention by excitable behaviour. The parents even pretend to be injured when danger threatens the eggs or young.

In October and November enormous flocks come over from the Continent and settle often for three weeks or a month in a particular field, which is usually resorted to yearly. In winter they wander about according to the weather, going wherever food can be found.

The upper parts of the bird are of a beautiful metallic green, the crown of the head and crest being almost black. Quills black, tipped with grey on the three outer pairs; tail feathers white, with a broad subterminal band of black on all save the outer pair; breast black; under tail coverts chestnut; rest of under parts white. In summer the chin and throat are black. In the female the crest is rather shorter and the outline of the extended wing is straighter. Length 12·5 in.; wing 8·75 in. The young bird has buff margins to the feathers of the upper parts.

LAPWING (*Vanellus vulgaris*)

Young (left)　　Adult, summer (right)

OYSTER-CATCHER (*Hæmatopus ostralegus*)

OYSTER-CATCHER

Hæmatopus ostralegus (Linnæus)

BRITISH resident. A common and abundant bird throughout the year on all our coasts, feeding more especially on mussels and limpets, which its powerful wedge-shaped bill enables it to detach from the rocks. Crustacea and marine insects are also eaten. Early in spring the large flocks begin to break up into pairs. Breeding takes place principally on our northern coasts; freely in Scotland and Ireland. Usually the eggs are laid early in May.

Generally, the nest is on shingle or the top of a low rock just above high-water mark, but where the rocks are steep and precipitous it is placed on the top of the cliff many feet above sea-level. In Scotland nests are sometimes made along river banks. The nest is merely a slight depression round which a few snails' shells or stones are laid. The eggs, two or three in number, are pale clay, freckled and spotted with black. Incubation is carried on by the hen, while her mate stands at some point of vantage from whence, on the approach of a stranger, he gives vent to his loud and noisy "keep, keep, keep". On hearing this alarm, the hen leaves her eggs and makes a chorus with her mate. The young when first hatched are dark greyish-brown, mottled and striped with black: they are at once taken to the shore and carefully watched over by the parents.

The head and neck, scapulars and mantle, lesser wing-coverts and tip of the tail are black, the rest of the plumage white. Bill orange-vermillion; legs pink. The sexes are alike, and in winter there is a white crescent round the top and front of the neck, and the bill is horn-coloured at the tip. The bill grows continually to counteract the wear and tear to which it is subjected. Length 16 in.; wing 9·75 in.

WOODCOCK

Scolopax rusticula (Linnæus)

BEST known in Britain from the vast numbers which arrive
during October to pass the winter with us. Although fairly well
distributed at this time, they are most abundant in Ireland and our
western counties. As the name implies, the Woodcock spends most
of its time in woods and plantations, flying every evening to wet
meadows and marshes where it feeds on worms and insects,
returning to the woods before daybreak. Early in March the vast
majority depart to their breeding grounds in northern Europe, but
some remain to nest with us. Breeding in this country has increased
in recent years.

The nest is a slight depression among dead leaves, generally at
the foot of a tree. The four eggs are yellowish-white, blotched
with ash-grey and reddish-brown. When the young are hatched
they are sometimes removed by the parents, the female being said
to carry them by holding them pressed closely to her body
between her legs. The eye is placed far back on the head, and the
external opening of the ear is placed forwards in front of and below
the eye.

The sexes are alike in colour: reddish-brown on the back,
vermiculated with dark brown. The under parts are drab, barred
with a darker shade. There is much individual variation in tint.
Length 14·29 in.; wing 7·5 in. The young resemble their parents,
but are rather more barred on the back.

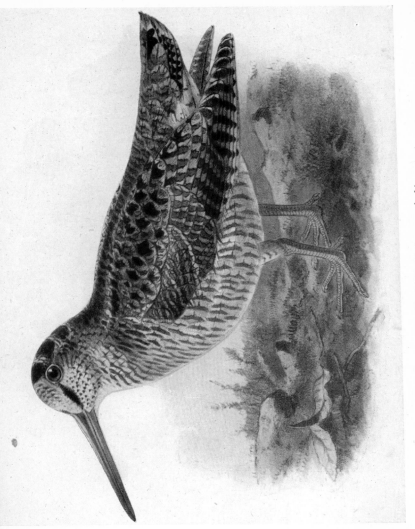

WOODCOCK (*Scolopax rusticula*)

Winter (above)   DUNLIN (*Tringa alpina*)   Summer (below)

DUNLIN

Tringa alpina (Linnæus)

AN abundant winter visitor to our coasts, frequenting estuaries, swamps, marshes and wet meadows, feeding on marine insects, worms and crustaceans. Generally seen in flocks which are often made up of thousands of individuals. When disturbed at one place they rise from the ground, twisting and turning in graceful flight, preparatory to settling again on some rich feeding ground. In summer many leave us to nest in northern Europe, while others betake themselves to inland moors or salt marshes round the coast on which to breed. It cannot be called a common nesting species with us, but it breeds in mountain areas in Scotland, Lancashire and Yorkshire, also sparingly in Devon and Cornwall.

The eggs are laid in May: the nest being a shallow scrape among heather, rough grass, or some other cover, and during the nesting season the male has a pretty little trill which he generally utters as he flies over the nest. The eggs, four in number, are pear-shaped, greenish-white, yellowish or brown with variable markings—spots, streaks and blotches of deep brown with underlying grey spots.

In winter the adult Dunlin is grey above and white below with a whitish bar across the extended wing. In spring the crown of the head is rufous, streaked with black. Mantle black, with broad rufous margins; the neck and throat white, streaked with black, breast black, belly white. The sexes are alike, the female being usually slightly the larger. Length about 7·5 in.; bill 1·7 in.; wing 4·5 in. But there is much variation in size. The young in autumn have the back nearly black, the feathers having narrow buff and rufous margins; the under parts are white, buff across the breast, and thickly spotted, especially on the lower breast, with black.

COMMON REDSHANK. *Totanus calidris* (*Linnæus*)

RESIDENT and a common breeding species in suitable localities.
Frequents the sea-shore, estuaries and marshy country. Feeds on
crustaceans, molluscs, worms and marine insects. The nest is made
in a shallow depression in the ground, in a tuft of herbage on the
beach, or in a rough, swampy pasture or moor. It is a slight matter
of grass and bents: sometimes hardly any material is used. The
four eggs, laid in April or May, are pear-shaped, rather large in
proportion to the size of the bird; light buff to warm yellow,
variously spotted and blotched with deep, or sometimes reddish
brown and with purplish-grey undermarkings. In winter the adult
is greyish-brown on the back; secondaries nearly white; rump and
under parts white, with a few dark streaks on neck and breast. Bill
black with red tip; legs red. In summer the upper parts are
yellowish-brown, barred and spotted with blackish, the under parts
white, profusely streaked on neck and sides of the breast with ash-
brown, the flanks being barred with the same colour. Length 11 in.;
bill 1·8 in.; wing 6·25 in. The female resembles the male. In the
young the legs are yellow.

SPOTTED REDSHANK. *Totanus fuscus* (*Linnæus*)

A RARE migrant, almost unknown in Scotland, Ireland and the
West of England, but a few are seen each year on passage in the
eastern counties. The bird breeds in the north of Scandinavia and
Russia, laying its eggs in dry situations at considerable distance
from its marshy feeding-ground. The young are taken to the
marsh as soon as hatched. In winter, and as seen in our country, the
upper parts are ash-grey with white mottling: under parts white.
Female rather larger than the male. Length 13 in.; wing 6·6 in.

SPOTTED REDSHANK
(*Totanus fuscus*) Young in autumn

COMMON REDSHANK
(*Totanus calidris*) Adult, summer

CURLEW (*Numenius arquata*)

CURLEW

Numenius arquata (Linnæus)

AN abundant resident throughout the United Kingdom. In the winter it is essentially a shore-bird, moving about in large flocks, which may be found in meadows and pasture-lands near the coast; these flocks journey to the shore twice daily to feed on the mud or rocks left bare by the ebbing tide. On the shore the food consists of small marine animals: inland, worms, spiders, snails, etc., are eaten. About April the bird leaves the coast to nest on heath-covered moors, and though it breeds in larger numbers in Scotland, where it is known as the Whaup, it is well distributed in the north and west of England and Ireland.

The nest is a shallow "scrape" with hardly any lining, situated among heather or in a grass field. The four eggs are pear-shaped, olive-green with prominent brown spots and blotches and purplish-grey undermarkings. Incubation is undertaken by both sexes.

An extremely wary bird, rising at the least alarm and calling out its loud "cour lie", which is heard from a considerable distance.

The general colour is a pale brown, with dark streaks; rump, vent and upper tail coverts white. In winter the under parts are very pale, almost white. The female is larger than the male, and the young in their first plumage are spotted rather than streaked on the back. The curved bill of this bird is a conspicuous feature: it is about five inches long, dark brown, yellowish at the base. The legs are bluish-grey. Length 21-26 in.; wing 11·5-12·25 in.

COMMON TERN

Sterna fluviatilis (Naumann)

OFTEN called Sea Swallow. Migrant. Winters in Africa. Arrives in Britain in May and nests in colonies round the whole of the coast as well as on some inland waters. Its food consists of small fish and crustacea which it catches after the manner of all Terns by dropping down on them with closed wings from a moderate height. The note is a sharp "kik-kik", but in the nesting season a loud and rather characteristic "ee-arre" is uttered.

The nesting colonies are on rocks, shingle beaches, near the margins of large inland waters, and on small islands where available. The eggs are laid in hollows of sand or shingle and are often overlooked because their colour harmonizes with surrounding pebbles. Sometimes a few bents or bits of seaweed are used as nesting material. When the nest is built inland in swampy places, a quantity of dried grass, etc., is used. The two or three eggs are variable, ranging from yellowish-white or greyish to deep buff or olive, blotched and spotted with brown and ash-grey. The young are covered with down and leave the nest as soon as hatched.

In summer the adult has the crown of the head and nape black, the rest of the back pearl-grey; rump white; tail feathers white with greyish outer webs. Under parts white tinged with grey. Bill orange-red with horn-coloured tip; legs coral red. Sexes alike. In winter the forehead is sprinkled with white and the under parts are nearly pure white. In their first plumage the young have the head white spotted with blackish-brown, the feathers of the back pearl-grey barred with buff or brown and tipped with white; but by late autumn the back is pure grey with the exception of a dark band along the carpal joint. Bill and legs yellowish. Length 14·25 in.; bill 1·7 in.; tail 6·5 in.; wing 10·5 in.

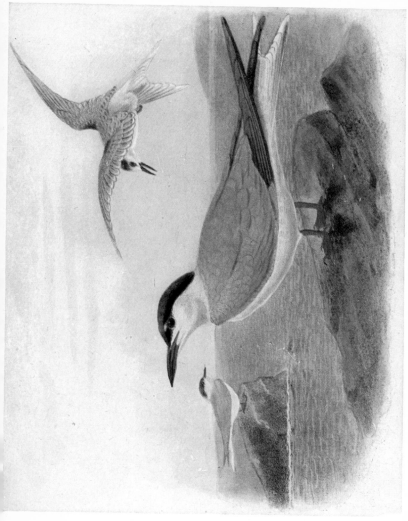

Summer

COMMON TERN (*Sterna fluviatilis*)

Young (flying)

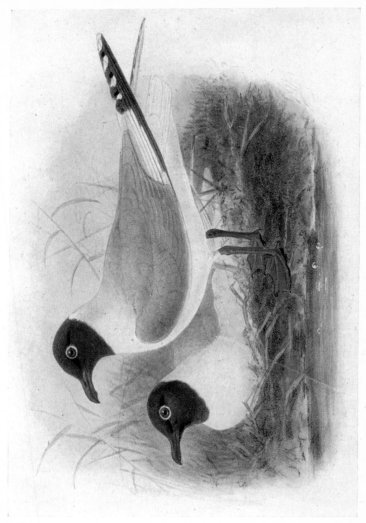

BLACK-HEADED GULL (*Larus ridibundus*)
Summer

BLACK-HEADED GULL

Larus ridibundus (Linnæus)

MISNAMED Black-headed, for the head is chocolate-brown. An abundant species throughout the United Kingdom. In autumn and winter it is seen all along the coast and up tidal rivers; in summer it resorts to inland marshes and bogs where it nests in great colonies. The bird is practically omnivorous. Inland, it follows the plough, feeding on worms and grubs thus laid bare; on the seashore, fish, crustacea, marine insects and garbage are greedily eaten.

The nest is a depression in the ground usually lined with dry grass and marsh plants. The three or four eggs are greenish, or of shades of buff and olive-green, with brownish-black spots and blotches and purplish undermarkings. The nesting season is April-May. The young leave the nest when two or three days old, but for a short time depend on their parents for food. They fly when about six weeks old. This gull is noisy at all times, but when the nesting ground is approached the babel of harsh screams is deafening. Although usually settling on the ground, this bird can perch with ease.

The sexes are alike: in winter they have the back pearl-grey, wing feathers white with dark margins to the inner webs, head white with two indistinct dark crescents connecting the eyes and ears respectively, rest of plumage white. In summer the head, with the exception of a narrow white circle over the eye, is dark brown. Bill, legs and feet carmine. The young in their first plumage are mottled with pale brown, but soon become like the adult except for a black bar on the tail and pale brown wing coverts. The characteristic plumage of the adult may not be assumed for three or four years. Length 16 in.; wing 12 in.

HERRING GULL

Larus argentatus (J. F. Gmelin)

BRITISH resident. Common round our coasts. Practically omnivorous, consuming fish, rats, crustacea and garbage thrown up by the tide. When it nests near colonies of Guillemots and Cormorants it systematically hunts the ledges and devours any uncovered eggs it can find.

This Gull nests in colonies, usually on ledges of precipitous cliffs, although small, low islets are sometimes chosen. The nest is made of grass, seaweed, and other vegetable débris. The two or three eggs are variable; various shades of buff, green or brown, with grey and deep brown spots, blotches and streaks. During the nesting season the bird is noisy and utters a variety of cries; at times the head is bent right down and suddenly thrown up in the air with a loud "ollick, ollick", which cry is taken up and repeated all over the colony.

In summer the adult has the mantle French grey, secondaries grey tipped with white, outer primaries black with white tips and large subapical "mirrors". Rest of plumage white. Bill yellow with red patch at basal angle. Legs flesh-coloured. In winter the head and neck are streaked with brownish. The young in the first autumn are mottled all over with pale brown. They do not become fully adult until their fourth year, though they sometimes breed in their third year. The adult plumage is assumed gradually and there is much individual variation both as regards the time and method in which it is assumed. Immature birds are seldom seen among colonies of adults during the summer, and it is somewhat doubtful where they spend the summer; possibly round some islets out at sea where food is plentiful. Length 24 in.; wing 17 in.

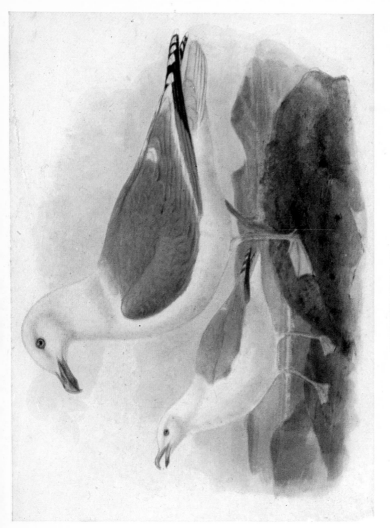

HERRING GULL (*Larus argentatus*)
Summer

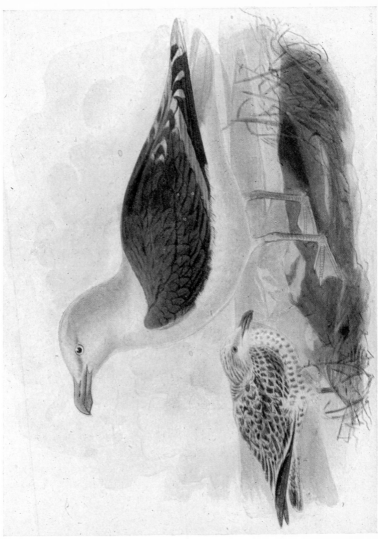

Summer (right)   GREATER BLACK-BACKED GULL (*Larus marinus*)   Young, first autumn (left)

GREATER BLACK-BACKED GULL

Larus marinus (Linnæus)

OUR largest Gull. Resident and may be seen during the winter on almost any part of our shores, but it is not so abundant as the Herring Gull. Breeds mainly in Scotland and on the west coast of Ireland, also in a few places on the south-western and western coasts of England. A bold and majestic species with a fine soaring flight, destructive to weakly lambs and young water-fowl. Its food consists largely of carrion and refuse of the shore. Although it has often been denied, this and other species of Gulls can completely immerse themselves and pick up food from the bottom in at least three feet of water. Having marked some food at the bottom, they rise to a height of about four feet and forcibly precipitate themselves into the water with half-open wings.

The pairs, about April or May, nest singly or in small colonies on rocks or islets, sometimes on the shore. The nest is a rough, badly constructed composition of seaweed, grass, etc. The two or three eggs are large and attractive; stone-colour, grey-brown or almost buff, blotched and spotted with brown or brownish-black with undermarkings of grey.

The usual note is a deep "ow, ow, ow". In plumage the adult has black back and wings tipped with white on the scapulars and secondaries; the rest pure white. The bill is yellow. Legs and feet flesh-coloured. Length 23 in.; wing 19 in. The young are mottled and barred with various shades of brown and buff, but are rather lighter in colour than those of the Herring Gull. The adult plumage is assumed in stages; occasionally it appears in the third summer.

KITTIWAKE GULL

Rissa tridactyla (*Linnæus*)

THE smallest British Gull. Common; frequents rocky coasts. Has a somewhat "squat" appearance owing to its short legs, and does not run on land so easily as some Gulls. It gets most of its food on the water and is rarely to be found among the flocks of Gulls that spend much of their time on the shore itself. Its food consists almost entirely of fish, in pursuit of which it dives and swims under water with ease.

It nests, from May to June, on the ledges of precipitous cliffs in immense colonies; in some cases the colonies must consist of many thousands. The nest is built of seaweed and other flotsam, and is often larger than the narrow cliff-ledge on which it is placed. The eggs, two or three in number, vary in ground colour from stone-colour to deep purplish-brown, and are variably blotched and spotted with reddish-brown or brownish-black. The shell has a rather rough texture. Both sexes take part in incubation. The young do not leave the nest until well able to fly.

In the adult the plumage is pure white on head, neck, rump, upper tail coverts and under parts. The mantle is dark lavender-grey. Scapulars and secondaries tipped with white. Primaries black, white-tipped. The legs and feet are black. The hind toe is absent and this helps us definitely to distinguish the bird at close quarters. In winter the nape and hind neck are grey like the mantle. Length 15·5 in.; wing 12 in. The young bird in its first autumn has the nape greyish but darker than in the adult, and the wing coverts and inner secondaries are thickly spotted with brownish-black.

Summer (below)   KITTIWAKE (*Rissa tridactyla*)   Winter (above)

Adult (left)   RAZORBILL (*Alca torda*)   Young (right)

RAZORBILL
Alca torda (*Linnæus*)

RESIDENT. Spends its time far out at sea in the Atlantic, never coming in sight of land except at the breeding season or when driven inshore by a winter gale. An expert swimmer and diver, though it flies well with rapid beats of its small wings. It feeds entirely on small fish. In April or May it assembles in colonies and nests on precipitous sea cliffs, particularly in Scotland, Flamborough, the Isle of Wight, Isle of Man, Lundy Island and Cornish and Irish coasts. A single egg is laid, preferably in some recess of the cliff where it is hidden, but if a recess is not handy an open ledge is used. There is no nesting material. The egg is variable in colour; ground yellowish-white, pale brown, reddish, sometimes bluish-green, spotted, blotched and streaked with reddish-brown.

The young bird when first hatched is covered with short down; it is blackish on the back, white beneath, and yellowish on the head. It remains in the nest about three weeks, after which it may be found swimming on the sea. At about two months the flight feathers begin to grow.

In summer the adult has the head, neck, chin, throat and back deep blackish-brown, a narrow line from the eye to the culmen white, and the rest of the under parts white. The bill is black and vertically flattened; it has two or more grooves near the tip that are whitish. It varies greatly in size, and is much larger in some individuals than in others, this difference being probably due to age. The sexes are alike, and in winter the chin and throat are white. Except in the size of the bill, the young bird resembles the adult after the first moult. Length 17 in.; wing 7·3 in.

COMMON GUILLEMOT

Uria troile (Linnæus)

BRITISH resident. In its habits, food and actions this species closely resembles the Razorbill, and they are usually found breeding on the same cliffs. Takes to the sea except in the breeding season, when colonies can be reckoned in thousands, the birds sitting as close together as possible.

This bird lays its egg on the bare open ledges of cliffs: it never seeks recesses like the Razorbill. The eggs are pronouncedly pear-shaped, a wise provision which prevents their rolling off the narrow ledges on which they are laid. Only one egg, which is variable, the ground colour being of various shades of cream, yellow, buff, blue and green; spotted, blotched and streaked with red-brown and black.

The young bird when first hatched is covered with iron-grey down on those parts of the body which are brown in the summer dress of the adult. The under parts are white and there are a few bits of white down on the head.

In summer, the adult has the upper parts, chin and throat dark brown, and the rest of the body white. The black bill is long, pointed and sharp, and not flattened as in the Razorbill. At the autumnal moult the brown on the chin, throat and back of the head is replaced by white, and in this and allied species all the flight feathers are moulted at the same time. Length 18 in.; wing 7·5 in.

The Guillemot flies rapidly but seemingly laboriously; its short wings have to be vibrated at considerable speed to keep the bird in the air. On land the bird is awkward, as a creature out of its element. It utters queer and eerie noises, some of them being reminiscent of the moaning of a person in pain.

Adult, summer (left)　　COMMON GUILLEMOT (*Uria troile*)　　Young (right)

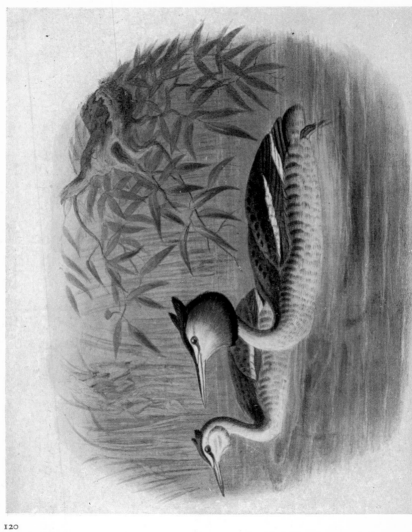

Adult, summer (right)   GREAT CRESTED GREBE (*Podicipes cristatus*)   Young (left)

GREAT CRESTED GREBE

Podicipes cristatus (Linnæus)

ALSO known as Greater Dabchick. A British resident, rather uncommon, but, owing to protection in recent years, it is increasing. In certain localities it is becoming common. In Scotland it breeds on several lochs as far north as Aberdeenshire. In Ireland it nests in several localities. It also breeds on inland waters in eastern and midland counties, and in Wales. The bird is found at all times of the year, but after the breeding season the majority leave their summer haunts on lakes, large ponds, etc., and may be found in the estuaries and bays along the coast.

The nest is a large floating mass of decaying vegetation generally well hidden among thick reeds, though occasionally it is placed in the open. The bird usually covers its eggs with damp vegetation when it leaves the nest. There are generally four eggs, which are yellowish-white when first laid, but they soon become stained to a dirty brown from contact with the nesting material. The young when first hatched are dark brown, longitudinally striped with white; they are carefully tended by both parents, who often carry them on their backs. The food consists of fish, crustaceans and any other living food which may be found. The bird is usually to be seen swimming about in the centre of open water. It flies well and strongly, appearing when on the wing rather like a duck.

In winter the plumage is dark brown above and white below, but in spring it assumes a chestnut tippet which surrounds the face; the crown of the head is dark brown, the cheeks and a stripe over the eye white. The female is rather duller than the male. The young in their first plumage are much like the adults in winter. Length 21 in.; wing 7·5 in.

RED-THROATED DIVER

Colymbus septentrionalis (Linnaeus)

A SEA-BIRD found along all our coasts in the winter months. In the breeding season it is restricted mainly to Scotland's northern and western isles: sometimes found in the west of Ireland. The elongate eggs, olive-brown spotted with umber, are laid close to the margin of a small secluded tarn or loch, or on an islet in a large loch. Little if any nesting material used—perhaps a few bents, bits of heather, or a few water-weeds. This bird feeds on fish and when it nests about waters which are fishless it journeys several miles to the sea or a large loch for food. The young leave the nest as soon as hatched, but at first are fed by the parents. If the sitting bird is disturbed it glides off the nest and dives into water without making a ripple, reappearing some distance away.

In winter the adult is brown on the back, with small white spots. The under parts are pure white : head and neck, on which the feathers are very downy, greyish-brown on the crown and nape, white on chin and throat. Legs, feet and bill blackish. The patch of chestnut-red on the throat, so noticeable in the summer, is lost in the winter, and in summer the white spots on the back do not occur. Sexes similar in plumage. Young birds in winter are distinguished by the white spots on the back being longer, tending to form arrow-shaped markings, and the feathers about the vent have narrow brown margins. Length of adult male bird about 23 in.; wing about 11 in. Female rather smaller.

RED-THROATED DIVER (*Colymbus septentrionalis*)
Adult in summer (right)   Young (left)

LEACH'S PETREL (*Oceanodroma leucorrhoa*)
(left)

STORM PETREL (*Procellaria pelagica*)
(right)